T0105814

THE ZION CULTURE

EASY READ SERIES

By Christopher G. E. Brodber
International Worship Ministries
36 Donhead Close, Paradise Heights, St. Michael,
Barbados, West Indies
Chrisbrodber@yahoo.com

*Our mission is to efficiently provide the world's finest, most comprehensive
book publishing service, enabling every author to experience success.
To find out how to publish your book, your way, and have it available
worldwide, visit us online at www.trafford.com*

Trafford rev. 11/16/09

All scripture references used are from the King James Version (KJV) of the Bible, unless

otherwise stated.

 www.trafford.com

North America & international
toll-free: 1 888 232 4444 (USA & Canada)
phone: 250 383 6864 ♦ fax: 812 355 4082

ACKNOWLEDGMENTS
AND THANKS

IT WAS A FEW DAYS after a twelve hour worship session entitled 'Freed To Worship', that the Lord shared with me truths about Zion. This book was written and based upon what I then learnt. I thank God for the opportunity to hear, and indeed also to be able to share.

I thank my Father, my Friend for His inspiring Word and His awesome presence.

Thanks to my wife Michele for being my 'chief cheerleader' and a true inspiration. I thank all the members of my family who were a source of encouragement. Special thanks to Erna Brodber and Velma Pollard, my aunts, and seasoned authors, for their contribution to this book.

I thank my editor, my former high school teacher, Sharon Knight, for her in-depth work on this project. Thanks also to Marcia Weekes, Director of Praise Academy of Dance, Barbados, for her encouragement.

Many thanks to you all who now take the time to read this book.

TABLE OF CONTENTS

Foreword .... *ix*

Preface .... *xi*

Introduction .... *xiii*

1   Blessed To Be a Blessing 1

2   A Unique Early And Latter Reign 8

3   Zion 18

4   A Culture Is Defined 26

5   Wisdom of The Culture 32

6   Local Transformation 43

7   Rebuilding Zion 58

8   Lift Up Your Heads 72

FOREWORD

AS AN ARTISTE, THOUGH MY area is prose fiction rather than music or poetry, I am delighted to see the place which Christopher gives to the arts in the transformation of our present challenged world. I have thought of my art as my sent ministry to the descendants of Africans enslaved in the New World, and have been a bit shy about my approach to art, but after reading Christopher's ZION CULTURE, I feel that my path is righteous, that I should continue on it unabashed and unapologetic; I feel a greater respect for what I do and feel emboldened to continue – but to do what I do better.

ZION CULTURE is not just encouragement for those who, like me, are currently involved in the arts, in consciousness-raising; it is a charge to all to explore their spiritual, their other selves, through the arts. A man who is quietly like David was in the wilderness, translating his visions into musical sounds, is not likely to be off cleaning a rifle for revenge; he is more likely to be hitting the barrel of the gun to see if he can find middle C. He will learn, too, from his love of the sounds that he can communicate with/to his neighbour through sounds rather than fists and bullets, and will want, in addition, to make the sounds which he creates, ones which he can share.

As this book has shown, King David of the Old Testament encouraged the arts, and he himself used it to mollify the demonic rage of Saul. Music in the therapy of the mentally disturbed is not unknown in psychiatric institutions today. It makes sense, as ZION CULTURE proposes, that today's leaders likewise encourage our violent populace to meditate, think and translate such meditations into positive communications. Let us all be singers and players of instruments. There are those who will say that the singers and players are already here: The Psalms to which Christopher refers us in this book are of a particular kind. They tend to be praise songs.

These, too, are well known to the culture which we brought to the Caribbean. Can we continue the tradition of giving praise and giving praise continually? All of us. For the social scientific framework in which this book is cast takes ZION CULTURE out of the narrow confines of the walled church into a wider world of living/levity.

Erna Brodber

Author: "Jane and Louisa Will Soon Come Home"

PREFACE

THE NATION OF ISRAEL HAS always been a nation under scrutiny. This is probably because the history of Israel is punctuated with great national successes as well as great national disasters. Not only has the nation's history provided the hope of all mankind, in Jesus Christ, but also many lessons on national development and social transformative strategies. Deep spiritual truths have originated from within the nation, providing powerful developmental principles for individuals and nations alike.

Israel seems to have had experiences on both ends of the pendulum as it relates to stability, economic prowess, population growth, military might and all the other areas of national development.

In this book we will take a look at a period in the history of Israel that provides a most powerful example for nations and individuals; a period in which the nation moved heaven with its transformative acts. Only the reign of King David could be credited for Israel's great transformation between kings Saul and Solomon.

Scripture reveals that God's intention has always been the great success and satisfaction of men. We will see that it is this purpose that caused the omniscient God to raise up David to serve his generation, and to present an example of a method of social reconstruction that brings prosperity and personal success.

We will see a unique strategy of development exposed, which the nation's leadership implemented to the unprecedented success of the people.

During the monarchy of King David, the nation established a unique and dynamic development strategy that had worked personally in the life of the king. The results were phenomenal and did the nation well. The system gave rise to the nation's wisest king and its most prosperous era to date.

We will see God use David, his government, and the people of the capital, as examples for all individuals and nations to follow. We will see the power of The Zion Culture in effect.

INTRODUCTION

A Prophecy
The Next Great Move

Luke 2:10
> *And the angel said unto them, Fear not: for, behold, I bring you good tidings of **great joy**, which shall be to all people. [emphasis added]*

EVERY EARTHLY OPERATION OF GOD is intended to increase the joy of men!

"Goodwill to all" is the passion of God!!!

As we pray "thy kingdom come, thy will be done on earth as it is in heaven", as taught by the Lord Jesus, we are facilitating an operation of God that sets bliss in place for humanity. God is always working to get men blessed!

Abundant life, love and liberty are God's passion for every individual on the face of this earth. When He says "seek me", He is saying seek the source of joy, seek the source of true satisfaction and peace; for He is the essence of every good thing and every good experience. There is no other way to have bliss, joy, and peace without a connection to the source; and the closer you are to God the more you get.

Closer to God is closer to excellence and every good virtue and experience. To distance ourselves from Him is to draw nearer to every negative experience.

God the Father sent His Son with the purpose of undoing the effects of the principles of contrary principalities; Jesus came to destroy every negative principle and its creator, the devil.

Jesus says,

John 10:10

> *The thief cometh not, but for to steal, and to kill, and to destroy: I am come that they might have life, and that they might have it more abundantly.*

It is God's purpose to give bliss on earth and in heaven. It is the devil's purpose to effect destruction and misery.

I perceive ....

As time winds down and many individuals anticipate varied futures for the earth and humanity, we will witness in the near future a new and phenomenal work of God manifesting in the lives of His people.

I prophesy ....

There shall be a great awakening that will take place within the Church, and its manifestations will bring tremendous increase in the Church's ability to reach the unsaved. There shall be a shift in the order of 'church'. There shall be an embracing of the 'spontaneous' and the use of the arts in an unprecedented manner.

The Church shall be washed in a period of renewal and refreshment by the power of the Spirit. The gift of discernment shall be resident and functioning in church leadership, to the liberty of congregations and nations alike.

A wind of God is about to blow on the souls of the redeemed, and the things that are minimized shall be maximized within the Church; the gifts that were in the background shall be placed in the foreground as time winds down.

At last the first commandment

From time immemorial the foremost answer to the world's woes has been, "Get closer to the source of all good things; get closer to the Creator God".

The foremost way of getting closer to God is by perfecting the performance of true worship; and the true worship is that which is passionately intimate and very expressive.

John 4:24
> *God is a Spirit: and they that worship him must worship him in spirit and in truth.*

The next great operation of God, indeed the last, before the rapture, I perceive, will be a great stirring within the hearts of believers for "in spirit" true worship. The world will witness the greatest manifestation of intimacy between the Church and her God.

John 4:23
> *But the hour cometh, and now*

is, when the true worshipers shall worship the Father in spirit and in truth: for the Father seeketh such to worship him.

I perceive and prophesy ....

The fulfilment of the first and greatest commandment of God will be the last 'move of God' upon the Church.

Matthew 22:37-38

Jesus said unto him, 'Thou shalt love the Lord thy God with all thy heart, and with all thy soul, and with all thy mind.

This is the first and great commandment.'

Before Jesus returns to the earth and time is no more, the Church will demonstrate passionate obedience to this commandment – and through the use of arts in intimate worship, creative expressions of love, strong verbalized appreciation and sincere devotion for God, true 'Davidic' type worship and praise shall erupt within the Church.

I perceive and prophesy ....

'Perfection of worship' before the rapture of The Bride. We will see phenomenal levels of the arts come to the fore within the Church, and we shall see its impact on individuals as well as nations.

It shall become evident that 'True Worshippers' are equipped with strategies, ideas, innovations, and creativity that can bring individual and national success.

This is the former king of Israel's testimony; it is David's story of empowerment unto success:

Psalm 89:19-21

Then thou spakest in vision to thy holy one, and saidst, I have laid help upon one that is mighty; I have exalted one chosen out of the people.

I have found David my servant; with my holy oil have I anointed him:

With whom my hand shall be established: mine arm also shall strengthen him.

Even so shall be the story of True Worshippers.

1
BLESSED TO BE A BLESSING

Fulfilling Promises to Abraham

GOD FOUND A CLOSE FRIEND in Abraham of Ur, and He chose to make His friend a promise:

Genesis 22:18

> *And in thy seed shall all the nations*
> *of the earth be blessed; because thou*
> *hast obeyed my voice.*

Israel was a nation to be specially and significantly blessed of God in order to fulfil this divine promise and purpose. The people were the descendants of Abraham, the 'seed' from whom all other nations were to be blessed. In order to bless these children of Abraham, the friend of God, and to make them a blessing to all others, God found an instrument, a tool to use to effect His plan: David the son of Jesse.

David was anointed and appointed of God to provide 'God's style' of leadership to Israel in order to get the nation to the intended place of success and prominence. Only a blessed Israel could bring a global blessing.

Genesis 12:2

> *And I will make of thee a great nation, and I will bless thee, and make thy name great; and thou shalt be a blessing.*

Israel's success was critical if it was to be a 'blessing' to the rest of the world, as was promised; so God inspired and influenced David to work a unique strategy on the nation of Israel to bring it to the place of international prominence.

God had said through the prophet Samuel, with regards to establishing David:

1Samuel 13:14

> *.... the LORD hath sought him a man after his own heart, and the LORD hath commanded him to be captain over his people.*

To Transform A Nation God Blessed A Man

The Lord selected and prepared David for the job of being head of state to Israel. Yet, David was not educated. He had no educational background that would have been comparable to modern-day higher learning or modern-day tertiary education. He had no technical training that would have been comparable to a present-day degree or doctorate. David was only a self-taught musician and a shepherd.

{How is God excited to use ordinary individuals to do extraordinary biddings! The Infinite mind still enjoys equipping the lowly to challenge and educate the finite minds. The foolish things of the earth God enjoys using as His raw material to confound the wise things. The rejected He enjoys making the perfected; for He brings from the dunghill and ash heap and sets them with princes.}

David was never the ordinary prudent selection as a candidate for leadership. As proven by Samuel's visit to Jesse to choose the next king, David never appeared typical, nor would he be a first or fourth choice for monarch.

He didn't have the physique or the form. He had no military training. He was not royalty and had no close relationship to anyone who was royalty. He therefore would have no chance to be educated as someone like Moses was.

There was nothing elite about David, nothing that would have made him look the candidate for leadership. David was a 'rough terrain' shepherd boy, who raised his father's sheep and practised music. Not a particularly 'kingly' combination. However, it seemed that somewhere within his humble background God's educational system was at work. The combination of musician and shepherd was God's way of preparing David for the job of head of state to His chosen people.

David's entrance to King Saul's palace was not on

the merit of an amazing defeat of Goliath, the Philistine champion, in battle. The victory may even have been considered by King Saul to be a fluke. David begins to associate with the nation's leaders and government by virtue of his musical skill, his ability to sing and play his instrument. He was only called on by the nation's leaders to provide a refreshing musical atmosphere and good entertainment for the king.

1 Samuel 16:17-18

> *And Saul said unto his servants, 'Provide me now a man that can play well, and bring him to me.'*
>
> *Then answered one of the servants, and said, 'Behold, I have seen a son of Jesse the Bethlehemite, that is cunning in playing, and a mighty valiant man, and a man of war, and prudent in matters, and a comely person, and the LORD is with him.'*

David's music administered to King Saul spiritual deliverance and comfort. Through his music David was actually doing a great service to the kingdom, to the entire nation of Israel. He was rescuing the king from spiritual oppression, ministering peace to the head of state under a divine enabling. David's abilities included sufficient power to defeat gigantic physical foes and to expel evil spirits.

Mighty music

Through his powerful ministry in music and song

David was not only rescuing the monarchy but, by extension, he was rescuing and sustaining the nation.

Where did this young man get such powerful music that ministered deliverance and exorcised evil spirits? David was operating in an anointing and ability outside of his age and era.

The ability to sing and play the way David did was the major part of God's leadership preparation. It was the strategic plan of God to educate and equip David with this artistic ability. David's music was not a hobby; it was specialized developmental training for leadership and prominence. It was the provision of revelation and understanding of true transformative power.

It was in order to bless Israel that God blessed David with a heart to worship; with talent, musical skills and sufficient time to practise and perfect his art. He was blessed with an anointing to become a 'True Worshipper'.

King Saul never realized that he was benefiting from David's training for leadership of the kingdom, but David's presence in the palace of Saul gave him a consciousness of what was to come; it mentally prepared David for a life of royalty and ultimate success.

It is apparent that his musical background facilitated a courage and faith that allowed David to be confident enough to take on boldly the challenges he would face in his life, the duel with Goliath included.

Not only was his unique training sufficient to give him confidence and faith to face a military 'giant' in combat, but it was enough to make him wise enough to win and gain respect and popularity in all Israel.

This playing of music had a powerful effect on the man's life, and was creating a prosperous future for him.

God's unique system of training was at work in David, and would soon be put to work in the nation itself. The system of 'True Worshipper empowerment' was being tested and proven in the life of David.

King of Praise

David rose to prominence, becoming king by virtue of that forged strength and wisdom from the passion for worship: The Lord's unique system of empowerment made David become the nation's leader.

As he experienced the rise to success, he was made king first over the people of the tribe of Judah. Providence, for Judah literally meant 'Praise' in Hebrew. Since he was the most proficient 'Praiser' in the land he should be king first in Judah.

Judah was separated from the rest of the nation of Israel at the time of David's becoming king there. David was to eventually inherit an Israel deeply divided, unstable and in a downward military and economic spiral. David reigned as king over Judah for seven years before his final ascension to prominence over the entire nation. He had established his leadership over Judah in Hebron and enjoyed a successful and stable reign over the tribe.

In the midst of David's successes, God ensured that it was public knowledge who and what David was, his true 'claim to fame'. He was "a sweet psalmist", a man inspired and empowered by the might of music, praise and worship.

2Samuel 23:1

*David the son of Jesse ... and the man who was raised up on high, the anointed of the God of Jacob, and the **sweet psalmist** of Israel ....*
[emphasis added]

2

A UNIQUE EARLY AND LATTER REIGN

Capturing Zion

Proverbs 28:2
> *For the transgression of a land many*
> *are the princes thereof: but by a man*
> *of understanding and knowledge the*
> *state thereof shall be prolonged.*

THE REIGN OF KING DAVID was uniquely different from
his predecessor. The nation of Israel became immediately
dominant within the region and truly successful under
his regime. There was a leadership method that David
was using to the immediate advancement of the nation.

Under David's reign the divided nation became

united again; such was the level of his influence on the people of the land.   When the nation was reunited, David removed his government from Hebron in Judah to a place northward, a fortified city location that was called **Zion.** He had conquered the city from the last pocket of Canaanite natives in that area, the Jebusites.

The Jebusites had held on to the land and put up strong resistance to every military campaign of Israel. They were 'a thorn in the flesh' to the nation, and a challenge to their faith. They presented a major problem to Israel, who was given a commandment from God to purge the land of the idolatrous inhabitants many years before. Yet, the Jebusites were quite comfortable and became more and more confident in their military ability to defend their land. They perceived that theirs was an impregnable fort and it would never be defeated or conquered by Israel.

It was spiritually significant that there was a stronghold on Zion. It is understandable that the enemy would endeavour to keep a hold on the location. The greatness of the future purpose and plans of God for the location must have been presumed.

{How Satan persistently seeks to defy faith, continuously trying to challenge God! How he seeks to stop the joy that God endeavours to bring to His people! In his efforts, however, he simply facilitates the omnipotence and omniscience of God being displayed. And every work of resistance amounts to an occasion being made for thanksgiving and praise to God for victory.}

However, these Jebusites should have long been displaced. Theirs was a last bastion of defiance in the

Promised Land, and Israel, prior to David, did not use its ability or power to remove them.

Exodus 34:11-15

> *Observe thou that which I command thee this day: behold, I drive out before thee the Amorite, and the Canaanite, and the Hittite, and the Perizzite, and the Hivite, and the Jebusite.*

> *Take heed to thyself, lest thou make a covenant with the inhabitants of the land whither thou goest, lest it be for a snare in the midst of thee:*

> *But ye shall destroy their altars, break their images, and cut down their groves:*

> *For thou shalt worship no other god: for the LORD, whose name is Jealous, is a jealous God:*

> *Lest thou make a covenant with the inhabitants of the land, and they go a whoring after their gods, and do sacrifice unto their gods, and one call thee, and thou eat of his sacrifice.*

God Himself had long purposed to work with the nation of Israel to purge the land, but He was never completely taken up on His offer. Finally, His trained servant, King David, enabled the power of heaven to manifest for the well-being of men. Demonic and Jebusite 'tooth-and-nail' struggle was not sufficient to stave off the plan of God. It would not be sufficient to resist the power of God that was an ally and ever available to David.

{How God enjoys wining battles against evil forces to the prosperity of men! He always is willing to fight for our joy and happiness; and yet men choose to ignore their greatest ally in their pursuit of happiness.}

David's preparation for leadership over Israel had involved displacing devils. He had first-hand experience in driving out evil spirits and was now versed in spiritual warfare, even before experiencing any physical warfare.

Zion was taken and the Jebusites were totally displaced. David displayed that he had the skill and ability to develop the nation on every front; he was able to deal with Israel's spiritual foes as well as its physical ones.

Wisdom at work

Zion was located on the borders of the tribes of Judah and Benjamin, and was now a strategic location for David's government. It would eventually form the most central part of the city of Jerusalem. Zion was neither in Judah proper nor in Israel, but was in a 'neutral' area. Its location was prudent so that there would be no contention between the people of Judah and Israel concerning prejudice in the chosen residential and governmental location of the king.

Zion became the 'City of David', where he established his home, his government and the capital of the nation. An immediate priority for David as he established the new capital was to empower the people by re-establishing the influence of God over the government and over the culture.

Psalm 21:1-3

> *The king shall joy in thy strength, O LORD; and in thy salvation how greatly shall he rejoice!*
>
> *Thou hast given him his heart's desire, and hast not withheld the request of his lips.*
>
> *For thou preventest him with the blessings of goodness: thou settest a crown of pure gold on his head.*

David understood that it was his specialized relationship with God through his artistic ability which brought him to prominence, and he was set on building a national strategy that utilized the power of the arts.

In order to do this David brought the Ark of the Covenant of God, which was the most significant possession of the nation, into the capital. It had been on the outskirts of Israel for 20 years. The Ark of the Covenant represented to all the people of Israel the presence of the Lord and His covenant of provision and protection over the nation.

2Samuel 6:15

> *So David and all the house of Israel brought up the ark of the LORD with shouting, and with the sound of the trumpet.*

David restored the ark to prominence again in the eyes of the people of Israel, and in doing so restored the desire for the presence of God to the people. He took it to the capital, signifying its importance to the nation's development and sustenance.

His leadership agenda would seem far from the ordinary. His efforts at affecting the faith and culture of his people, as opposed to some direct effort at building the economy and military, to onlookers would seem a sign of poor leadership skills but, of course, David was not the usual.

The Tabernacle of David

David built a unique tent for the ark. It was called the 'Tabernacle of David'. David himself got involved with the design and construction of the tent, the place for the centrepiece of the people's faith.

This project was of extreme priority for the king if the kingdom was to be strong and successful. This tent/ tabernacle, housed the Ark of the Covenant for over 30 years, before the eventual construction of the more permanent walled temple by David's successor, his son, King Solomon.

The original tent that Moses had built for the ark in the wilderness long before was still in existence at the point of David's erecting the new tabernacle.

1Chronicles 21:29

> *For the tabernacle of the LORD,*
> *which Moses made in the wilderness,*
> *and the altar of the burnt offering,*
> *were at that season in the high place*
> *at Gibeon.*

David had a great revelation and a particular purpose that was to surpass the design of the original Tabernacle of Moses. His revelation concerned public access to the ark - the presence of God. He intended to make sure it was in a central location, accessible to all God's people, for inspiration and encouragement.

David had all the people get involved in the initial process of bringing up the ark into the capital. He made it a national event: the procession of God's presence to the nation's capital.

2Samuel 6:17

> *And they brought in the ark of the LORD, and set it in his place, in the midst of the tabernacle that David had pitched for it: and David offered burnt offerings and peace offerings before the LORD.*

The Tabernacle of David was significantly and uniquely different from the former tabernacle. The Tabernacle of Moses was built with veils which, apparently, were not present with the Tabernacle of David. The Tabernacle of Moses had strong, restrictive religious rituals that prevented the 'ordinary' Israelite from approaching the ark. Under Moses the ark was set in the centre of the people, who encamped around it at a distance and could not come near to it. Only those of the tribe of Levi had access to the tabernacle and to the ark.

David's tabernacle was now at the centre of the location of the Israelite Government. It signified God's influence over the monarchy, and His pre-eminence over the nation. It signified that He was the guide and the pride of Israel. This change obviously affected and influenced the people and the culture.

The ark and the tabernacle became a significant

inspiration to the nation, as it had once been in their past, motivating the people during battle.

> 1 Samuel 4:5
> *And when the ark of the covenant of the LORD came into the camp, all Israel shouted with a great shout, so that the earth rang again.*

Passing on passion

From the transporting of the ark, to its arrival and placement within the tabernacle, the people of Zion and Israel saw the king's passion. They saw that their head of state held the ark of God's presence with deep respect and reverence. They observed a display of true love, and an ongoing real relationship with David and his God. They saw that David had brought 'the presence of God' into the very location where he lived and worked. The people witnessed a passion in the king, an unfeigned love for God. They noticed that he expressed his love for God freely and with all his might. They had been aware of his music and singing, but they would now see its source and its purpose.

David held nothing back of his music, singing and dancing, whether in public or in private. He was pleased to allow the people to witness him worshipping wholeheartedly. This was the nature of their king.

Psalm 9:1-2

> *I will praise thee, O LORD, with my whole heart; I will show forth all thy marvellous works.*
>
> *I will be glad and rejoice in thee: I will sing praise to thy name, O thou most High.*

They observed their king regularly express his love to God, openly and passionately, through the use of the arts. David danced, sang, played on instruments and wrote songs. He displayed before the people what he had learnt and knew about God: God loves music; God Himself sings; He enjoys worship and praise; He is Himself passionate and enjoys when His people are passionate and expressive.

Zephaniah 3:17

> *The LORD thy God in the midst of thee is mighty; he will save, he will rejoice over thee with joy; he will rest in his love, he will joy over thee with singing.*
>
> *The best and most valuable sacrifice to give to God was demonstrated by the king to be an offering of worship and praise. The king regularly made these kinds of 'revolutionary' offerings to God, and the people took note.*

Psalm 54:6

> *I will freely sacrifice unto thee: I will praise thy name, O LORD; for it is good.*

Psalm 107:22
> *And let them sacrifice the sacrifices of thanksgiving, and declare his works with rejoicing.*

David knew that music is the creative creation of the Creator, as are colours and scents, and that it finds its best expression when played in honour of the One who created it; for as it is played to the Creator He will educate the one playing as to new, creative, true ways of playing His music. Dance, passionate dance, David knew to be the most appropriate way of honouring music; poetry was the most appropriate way of honouring words – for the arts find their true expression and true context when ministered to the One who created them.

{Because the 'Sons of music and arts' have not understood their heritage, the world, the secular scene, has been the one to most explore its uses. From the world's exploration of the arts, they have appeared to be the masters of it – of music, dance, poetry, song writing, etc. Yet, they are not the heirs. The Believers are, and they are to be the masters.}

3

ZION

Liberating the People

DAVID HAD HIS GOVERNMENT IN Zion and it was here he planned to initiate the strategy. He would have recalled the process that brought his exaltation; his liberty and opportunity to explore his gifts and talents; the occasions in the wilderness of playing to God and finding himself, in and through God's presence. He obviously desired the same experience for the people, for the nation.

So King David commanded the people to "Sing!" It became a commandment from both David and the Lord to the people. David fully expected and encouraged all of the people to sing. He legislated it as a part of his strategy. Singing unto God would be done continuously at the tabernacle.

Psalm 33:1-3

> *Rejoice in the LORD, O ye righteous: for praise is comely for the upright.*
>
> *Praise the LORD with harp: sing unto him with the psaltery and an instrument of ten strings.*
>
> *Sing unto him a new song; play skilfully with a loud noise.*

Dancing was also promoted - it was a decree of the king.

Psalm 149:1-3

> *Praise ye the LORD. Sing unto the LORD a new song, and his praise in the congregation of saints.*
>
> *Let Israel rejoice in him that made him: let the children of Zion be joyful in their King.*
>
> *Let them praise his name in the dance: let them sing praises unto him with the timbrel and harp.*

The playing of instruments, the writing of songs and the writing of poetry all became a responsibility of the people. It was a zealous, joyful commission from the king for the people to pursue the exploration of their gifts and talents. It was not a commission for a new religious, ritualistic deadness of expression. It was a commission to have fun exploring their individual abilities. It was permission to be creative and innovative. It was a challenge to the people to allow the Lord to help them discover their individuality, and to express their deepest emotions.

David ensured that the capital of Israel was transformed into a city of praise; a city filled with the passionate use of arts. He had the Ark of the Covenant and the uniquely constructed tabernacle there as inspiration for the people as they practised their music, singing and dancing, and played unto the Lord their God. He was strategically following the Lord's system for development, which had worked in his own life.

{How many people do not know who they are because they have never taken the time to explore themselves? They choose to explore issues and others, and hardly ever feel confident enough to explore themselves. How many have gone to miserable graves, because they never took the opportunity to be free? They never allowed the Lord to shine a light on their souls to release and reveal their deepest emotions.}

Psalm 50:2

> *Out of Zion, the perfection of beauty,*
> *God hath shined.*

Changing the culture

The arts became the vehicle of change in Zion. The present prevailing perception is that the artistic expressions of a people will only come to the fore when the economy sets them free. It is believed that a successful economy will give rise to passionate artistic expression. Financial success will give the people the motivation and freedom to be creative and to explore the arts.

David didn't think so; he was engineering successful artistic expression to give rise to a successful economy and nation. He perceived that a passionate, praising people would be motivated and driven to build a strong nation. He perceived that the nation's economy would be affected once the people were liberated to experiment with their gifts. David knew that the people's faith would bring them focus and a unity of purpose.

He ensured that the people were aware of his own passion, and he encouraged them to be passionate too. He demonstrated his commitment to the arts, and instructed that the people also use their gifts – singing, dancing, songwriting and poetry – to praise and worship their God.

The atmosphere of the fortress city, Zion, was charged with freedom of expression, passion and creativity. Everywhere the sound of music could be heard. The choreographers of dance were at work; the musicians were practising, teaching others, and tuning their instruments. The songwriters were busy writing psalms and songs. The city was abuzz daily with the purpose of full expression of devotion to God through the diligent use of the arts.

Consider the energy of the land. Cymbals clashing on street corners, drum numbers being practised behind buildings, flutes and harps sounding late at night to candlelight, singing being heard in homes – all a concerted effort to offer the best sounds and sights to bless God.

David had caused a revolution in the minds and spirits of the people. He had initiated a 'revival'. The people delighted in their beliefs, and found true inspiration from their religion. Their main sacrifice to God was now to be their gifts, their skills, their talents, instead of animals and birds. They were aware that they themselves were the deep desire of God. He delighted in their talents, in their dancing and singing. Therefore, what was offered constantly to God at the Tabernacle of David was the passion and creativity of the people. They did not do away with animal sacrifice; it was still a part of their faith. But the greater sacrifice they esteemed was the sacrifice from their artistic expressions of love to God.

> Psalm 27:6
>> *And now shall mine head be lifted up above mine enemies round about me: therefore will I offer in his tabernacle sacrifices of joy; I will sing, yea, I will sing praises unto the LORD.*

The people had embarked on a new way of ministering to the Lord; a new system of making an 'offering' to their God. They played their music, sang their songs, and danced their dances continually unto the Lord, for the sole purpose of His enjoyment.

The Children of Zion

Even the children would have been involved in the celebrations of the arts. They, too, would have been encouraged and supported in using their gifts and talents. The dancing and singing of children would have added another dimension of power to the atmosphere of Zion.

Psalm 8:2
>> *Out of the mouth of babes and sucklings hast thou ordained strength*

> *because of thine enemies, that thou*
> *mightest still the enemy and the*
> *avenger.*

David would have known to allow the children to go before the Lord, for they more readily display their creativity than adults. They have less fear and care nothing of reputation, or of being ridiculed and so the children could offer the 'purer' praise. The children would sing their songs and dance their dances with a liberty that the adults would struggle to emulate; and so they would be clearer channels for inspiration and new deposits from God of creative expression.

The children, by the innocence of their offerings, would contribute considerably to the energy of the atmosphere of Zion. For the secret of David's strategy was perfected in the children, for the strategy in essence was a call to the nation to be childlike in expressing their God-given natural gifts and talents.

New Testament Attitude in an Old Testament Age

David caused Zion to become a city operating under a Romans 12v.1 revelation.

> *I beseech you therefore, brethren, by*
> *the mercies of God, that ye present*
> *your bodies a living sacrifice, holy,*
> *acceptable unto God, which is your*
> *reasonable service.*

There was a clear New Testament atmosphere in this Old Testament age.

David's revelation facilitated the people's coming near to God's presence by faith. Faith that they would be accepted, faith that they would not perish, faith that they were loved by God, and that He delighted in them more that in animals and birds.

It was a revolutionary thinking. Moses had alluded to the concept, Miriam had operated on the fringes of the idea with her expressions of dance, but now the City of Zion was manifesting it.

David had learnt the lessons of the power and relevance of faith. He had learnt the importance of a sincere relationship with God as opposed to religious ritual.

Before becoming king he had eaten bread that was religiously laid up for the priests to eat, and forbidden for 'common men' to eat. He had eaten the 'shewbread' of the Tabernacle of Moses in faith, believing that God loved him and knew his heart, and that he would not be condemned for this break in religious routine.

Matthew 12:3-4

> *Have ye not read what David did, when he was hungry, and they that were with him;*
>
> *How he entered into the house of God, and did eat the shewbread, which was not lawful for him to eat, neither for them which were with him, but only for the priests?*

David's faith was based on his relationship with God, and not the merit of religious routines. This was the very principle he was sowing into the nation's culture; and he began at the City of Zion.

He had personally danced with all his might before the Lord, even so that his undergarments were revealed. This was 'irreligious' and a great offence under the former revelation and system of religious rite. Yet, David thought nothing of this as he had obtained a fuller revelation and an understanding of what God really delights in. David realized that friendship with God was superior to servitude, and that God doesn't see as man sees.

He understood that God truly looks at the heart, and is not offended if the heart is right and true love is the driving motive. David taught these things to the people. They understood and emulated it; they believed that passionate praise was pleasing to God.

Israel had only known religious routine, which they had inherited from the Tabernacle of Moses. They understood 'distant' religious practices, and had never majored in a living, personal and individual relationship with their God.

But David went about the task of stirring the hearts of the people of Zion to be personal and intimate with their God. For passionate and creative music and dance made their relationship with God personal. Therefore, inspiration, revelation and visions would come from God, even as they ministered their gifts, their sacrifices of the arts to God. They were inspired as they ministered to God, and so their energy and the joy and the zeal would be perpetuated.

Psalm 84:7

> *They go from strength to strength, every one of them in Zion appeareth before God.*

4

A CULTURE IS DEFINED

Holy Land

THE HOLY LAND IS A title used for the land of Israel because of the unique relationship that the people had with God. Israel is also called the Holy Land because of promises God made with regards to the land.

Israel's dynamic history, which most notably includes the birth of the Lord in Bethlehem, is also reason for the term 'Holy Land'. Jesus' ministry of teaching and miracles, His death, burial and resurrection, were also there in Israel – all reasons behind the term 'Holy Land'. Now, we can add the Zion Culture to this notable history, since the experience with the Zion Culture seemed to have been the zenith in Israel's national cooperation with God.

National behaviour

Geographically, Zion was the summit of Israel's Mount Hermon, but spiritually, Zion seemed the summit of Israel's culture and relationship with God.

A culture is a particular society at a particular time; the taste in art and manners that are favoured by a social group, or the attitudes and behaviour that are characteristic of a social group. Zion, through the effort and revelation of the king, became a most unique place on earth. It became a place with a people of a culture of passion, of expressive and liberal use of the arts.

David led the way and laid a strong example for the people of the city.

He is accredited with having written over 73 of the psalms that exist in the Bible, as he led the way in passion, zeal, expressiveness and creativity in the worship and praise of God. He demonstrated true freedom of expression and heartfelt devotion to God.

2Samuel 6:14

> *And David danced before the LORD with all his might; and David was girded with a linen ephod.*

David motivated the people by continually writing songs and playing music, showing that "if the head of state can, you can too".

1Chronicles 16:7

> *Then on that day David delivered first this psalm to thank the LORD into the hand of Asaph and his brethren.*

The people of Zion responded by emulating the king's zeal and passion for God.

Because of the power of the culture and the people's passion; because of the use of the arts by the people, the very name of the city became famous throughout the then world, and remained famous through the ages, even to this present day.

The name 'Zion' began to refer to a people of God; a people close to the heart of their God. It represented a powerful and unique place where there was a strong relationship between God and the people. It was a mysterious place, held in awe by all who heard of the goings-on there.

The name 'Zion'

Many religious and secular groups today have used the name 'Zion' because of its appeal. Mormons have called their place of utopia Zion. Rastafarians have called their eternal home in Ethiopia Zion. Hollywood, too, has jumped in; the popular movie, 'The Matrix', calls the last human city that must be defended at all costs Zion. Not to mention the numbers of streets, avenues and townships which now bear the name Zion.

The name 'Zion' has also been used synonymously with the entire Jerusalem, and is interchangeable with the New Testament Church. The name now represents the place where God is most to be found on earth. It speaks of a place where God's attention is, a place where He has a constant covenant and connection. The name is even used as synonymous with heaven itself.

Indeed, Zion represents a geographic location that

God has covenanted to bless eternally. All recognition and sacredness of the place came from the passion of its inhabitants. They got God's attention and made the geographical place a delight to God. The city became special to God because the people and their way of life were special to God.

Psalm 87:2

> *The LORD loveth the gates of Zion*
> *more than all the dwellings of Jacob.*

The Lord had found a people, a culture, that were expressive to Him – open, and sacrificing of their time, their energy, their gifts – to show their love and excitement and appreciation for Him. There was no other nation on earth that would offer themselves as wholeheartedly as the people of Zion. He saw the attitude of David, whom He had called "a man after my own heart", sown into the people.

The land and the people therefore were favoured by God, as was David. God blessed the people even as they blessed Him.

Psalm 65:1

> *Praise waiteth for thee, O God, in*
> *Sion: and unto thee shall the vow be*
> *performed.*

Many nations count their chief assets as the people and the land. Yet for Zion and Israel their chief asset was their unique spirituality and their relationship with the living God. It was this spiritual relationship which enabled their land to be most blessed.

Eden and Zion

Because of the culture, Zion became in the spirit what the Garden of Eden was in the physical. The Garden of Eden was a revered 'spot of heaven' on earth. It was designed to offer man a physical place of paradise similar to the spiritual paradise of heaven. The man that God had put in the garden was given the duty to keep and recreate the garden, filling the earth with the same bliss and beauty. Flowers and trees that brought magnificent beauty, fruit trees that were delightful were all a part of Eden's landscape, which was to spread throughout the entire earth.

Genesis 1:28

> *And God blessed them, and God said unto them, 'Be fruitful, and multiply, and replenish the earth, and subdue it ...'*

Yet, while Eden was a replica of heaven in its physical landscape, Zion became a replica of the atmosphere of heaven – the beauty of the sound of music, the continuous, glorious singing, the beauty of the freedom and passion of worship and praise. Those glories that exist in the music of heaven were being replicated on the earth by the people of the Zion culture – the joy, the gladness, the playing of instruments continually, and the spontaneous worship and praise.

Even as the Lord walked comfortably in the cool of the day in Eden, He must have been well pleased to operate amid the celebrations and singing of the Zion Culture. The rich atmosphere would have been amicable to God, who enjoys residing in continuous sounds of music.

Psalm 22:3

> `*But thou art holy, O thou that inhabitest the praises of Israel.*

5
WISDOM OF THE CULTURE

The Blessings in Zion

THE ZION CULTURE SIGNIFICANTLY AFFECTED the nation of Israel. The geography/topography of Israel would have been impacted because God blessed the land. It was already promised to be a fruitful land, described as flowing with milk (that is, all agriculture in the sense of animal rearing and farming would prosper) and honey (a place of choicest and chief blessings and sweet provision), but now a new dimension of God's favour and blessings was poured upon the land. Because of the new relationship the people had with their God, every sphere of the national life would be affected.

Because there was now a culture of the arts, the benefits of the arts would have been manifested in the social composition of the nation. The primary benefits, of course, were the spiritual blessings derived from the culture. Where God is blessing, social transformation occurs.

It is impossible to experience true spiritual blessings and not experience other blessings as well, for God satisfies the 'whole man'.

1 Thessalonians 5:23
> *And the very God of peace sanctify you wholly; and I pray God your whole spirit and soul and body be preserved blameless unto the coming of our Lord Jesus Christ.*

The social make-up of the nation would have begun to change as the people became free to express themselves to God, free to use their talents and gifts to please God. They became a confident and bold people.

Psalm 9:10-11
> *And they that know thy name will put their trust in thee: for thou, LORD, hast not forsaken them that seek thee.*
>
> *Sing praises to the LORD, which dwelleth in Zion: declare among the people his doings.*

Timidity and bashfulness would not have been a common occurrence in this empowered people. As they developed the sense of individualism, they developed a sense of strength and personal worth. They perceived their own unique value, and their own unique purpose.

They felt their own part in the 'big picture', the 'great scheme' of things.

There would have been minimal fear in the people. The reality of being able to come in faith to the presence of God would have given them the courage to do anything and to go before anyone; they would have perceived, 'if God be for us, who can be against us'?

> 2Samuel 21:18-21
>
> *And it came to pass after this, that there was again a battle with the Philistines at Gob: then Sibbechai the Hushathite slew Saph, which was of the sons of the giant.*
>
> *And there was again a battle in Gob with the Philistines, where Elhanan the son of Jaare-oregim, a Bethlehemite, slew the brother of Goliath the Gittite, the staff of whose spear was like a weaver's beam.*
>
> *And there was yet a battle in Gath, where was a man of great stature, that had on every hand six fingers, and on every foot six toes, four and twenty in number; and he also was born to the giant.*
>
> *And when he defied Israel, Jonathan the son of Shimea the brother of David slew him.*

The very same courage that David had as he faced bears and lions, and the confidence he had to face

Goliath, was now operating in the people on a national level. They would be timid before no one. God was well pleased with them and they therefore perceived that they could accomplish anything.

The people constantly exercised their creative skills as they prepared songs or dances, and created instruments and played their music. This would facilitate a willingness to be creative in other areas and facets of life. They were a people now versed in being creative and expressive. Their innovation would affect their businesses. It would affect their jobs, their communities, their homes, and it would even affect their relationships.

Psalm 33:12

> *Blessed is the nation whose God is the LORD; and the people whom he hath chosen for his own inheritance.*

The people would have been abuzz with creativity and ideas, as they expressed their faith passionately through the arts to God. Their singing, music, songwriting, dancing, all affected their social structure and their thinking – individually and corporately. Their singing would have even affected their health, their physical bodies. Psalm 91 became the experience of the people.

Psalm 91:9, 14, 16

> *Because thou hast made the LORD, which is my refuge, even the most High, thy habitation;*
>
> *Because he hath set his love upon me, therefore will I deliver him: I will set him on high, because he hath known my name.*

> *With long life will I satisfy him, and*
> *shew him my salvation.*

Researchers have indicated that singing strengthens the immune system, and relieves stress.

Researchers have declared that singing is good exercise for the lungs, and that it tones up intercostal muscles and the diaphragm.

Singing is said to improve an individual's sleep, and decreases muscle tension. The circulatory system and the heart benefits from an individual's singing. The sinuses and respiratory tubes are opened up, for a healthier life. It is said that singing can reduce anger, depression and anxiety, which can all result in a longer, healthier, and happier life.

The arts

Scientists say that singing increases self-esteem and confidence. It increases a sense of well-being, promotes bonding, and even increases understanding and empathy between one culture and another.

Singing creates a forum for sharing, and encourages a sense of community; it also provides a great opportunity for fun among friends. David's institutionalizing of public singing would have facilitated these benefits for the people of the Zion Culture.

Not only was "Sing!" a command for the inhabitants of Zion from their king, but the people were instructed and encouraged to play music as well.

There are several benefits to playing music. Playing

music helps develop the left side of the brain that is responsible for processing language. Those who play an instrument learn craftsmanship, teamwork and a sense of discipline and commitment. Playing an instrument gives an individual an important forum for self-expression. As one performs on an instrument, one apparently is learning to conquer fear and to take risks.

It is evident today that secular science esteems music, whether governments and policymakers do or not. Some educational institutions, perceiving the benefits of music, have included the playing of instruments in the curriculum of their schools. Secular science has declared that those students who study the arts achieve high grades during their school years.

Dancing brings its own benefits to the dancer as well. Dancing is said to change the mental outlook, giving a sense of creativity, giving motivation and a sense of energy. Dancing provides a unique outlet for the expression of self through movement. Dancing is a health booster as well, through calorie burn-offs and weight control. The dancer's heart and circulatory system benefit from dancing.

David's strategy institutionalized singing, the playing of instruments, dancing and songwriting, all to the benefit of the people and the success of the nation.

Psalm 149:2-5

> *Let Israel rejoice in him that made him: let the children of Zion be joyful in their King.*
>
> *Let them praise his name in the dance: let them sing praises unto him with the timbrel and harp.*

> *For the LORD taketh pleasure in his
> people: he will beautify the meek with
> salvation.*
>
> *Let the saints be joyful in glory: let
> them sing aloud upon their beds.*

The fear of the Lord

Passionate praise, passionate worship, expressive dance and creative song-writing would have been constant practices of the Zion Culture. As the city's culture adopted this constant joyful faith, they would have benefited from factors unknown to them. They would have received strength and inspiration, and so much more, as they expressed themselves to God daily.

Their faith benefited their everyday lives in a tangible and real way. There would have been unity and joy in the streets, in the homes, and in the nation's capital.

Psalm 68:24-26

> *They have seen thy goings, O God;
> even the goings of my God, my King,
> in the sanctuary.*
>
> *The singers went before, the players
> on instruments followed after; among
> them were the damsels playing with
> timbrels.*
>
> *Bless ye God in the congregations,
> even the Lord, from the fountain of
> Israel.*

David had institutionalized in a living way a national

faith. He had been successful at causing a unity of vision and purpose among the people, through this common expression of the arts.

The faith of the people, called in their times "the fear of the Lord", would have been a joy and not a burden. It would have brought happiness and not drudgery. Relating to God would have replaced religious 'mechanical' routine. The hearts of the people were now open to their God, expressing their love and trust in Him regularly, and enjoying His rich presence.

Their faith facilitated a unique wisdom. It is evident that as strong faith develops, wisdom increases, because the individual now has a correct perspective on the world, a correct platform from which to develop other thoughts. When faith is present then a basic logic for understanding natural laws of existence exists. The "fear of the Lord", active faith in God, is the "beginning of wisdom". The fear of the Lord also gives strong confidence. When you believe in the existence of God and have taken the opportunity to adjust your life to the convictions of faith, strong confidence in the performance of whatever the duty or chore will result.

Proverbs 10:27

> *The fear of the LORD prolongeth days: but the years of the wicked shall be shortened.*

David's successor – his son, King Solomon – called the wisest man to ever live, was a product of the Zion Culture. He would have been inspired by the atmosphere that saturated Zion. It is out of his relationship with God that he would have been granted the great wisdom for which he is renowned. As a resident of Zion and one influenced by the culture, he penned the Songs of Solomon, and most of the book of Proverbs. He was poetic and artistic, for he was a recipient of the "fear of the Lord" prevailing in Zion.

A healthy city

The joy and expressiveness of true faith among the people facilitated a blessing. They were blessed spiritually, emotionally, physically, psychologically and financially, for happy people are productive and innovative people. God was on their side and he was willing to make the world know it. The people would have enjoyed a greater state of health due to their spirituality. Though the nation experienced a plague due to David's census in his latter years, viruses and plagues generally would have been minimal in the land, as God had originally promised.

Exodus 23:25

> *And ye shall serve the LORD your God, and he shall bless thy bread, and thy water; and I will take sickness away from the midst of thee.*

The powerful early promises to the nation would have been made manifest in Zion. The sustaining power of God, which only their foreparents had known in the wilderness, would now have been the experience of the people. They were protected by angels, borne up in their hands, kept from the woes in the world.

Psalm 91:10-12

> *There shall no evil befall thee, neither shall any plague come nigh thy*

dwelling.

For he shall give his angels charge over thee, to keep thee in all thy ways.

They shall bear thee up in their hands, lest thou dash thy foot against a stone.

A strategy for all

The strategy that David used to bring about this state of blessedness of the state was a strategy that could work with any people of any nation, once they executed the same joys, passion and faith in offering their gifts and talents to God. The blessings of the institutionalized use of the arts would work with any people who turned wholeheartedly to God.

There is hardly any person who would say they do not like music, or that they do not like to dance. It is because God Himself has deposited in everyone the desire to do that which will get them most blessed, and bring them into true satisfaction and fulfilment. For the very hearts of men beat with a rhythm; we were all created unto music and dance.

Music has power with men because of its created purpose. The very babe on the breast responds to music, and as early as possible they naturally begin to dance. And music is used to educate children for basic learning of numbers and letters, because of its appeal to the mind.

David institutionalized for Israel that which was actually a human need – the freedom of expression, liberty to dance, to sing, to create with purpose and direction, to enjoy music. The satisfaction of this human desire made Zion and, by extension, Israel, a happy and healthy place.

Proverbs 17:22
> *A merry heart doeth good like a medicine: but a broken spirit drieth the bones.*

Psalm 89:15-16
> *Blessed is the people that know the joyful sound: they shall walk, O LORD, in the light of thy countenance.*
>
> *In thy name shall they rejoice all the day: and in thy righteousness shall they be exalted.*

THE ZION CULTURE

6

LOCAL TRANSFORMATION

The Power of Culture

MANY CULTURES EXIST, WITH THEIR particular strengths and weaknesses. There are cultures that have serious negative effects on their society, and operate to the detriment of the people. There are cultures as well that function to the detriment of the land.

The former inhabitants of Canaan, that geographical area that Israel now occupied, operated with counterproductive cultures. The land was inhabited by different nations of peoples before Israel settled there. The Jebusites, the Armorites, the Girgasites, the Hivites, and several other peoples had their boundaries within the geography of Canaan.

Genesis 10:16-18

And the Jebusite, and the Amorite, and the Girgasite,

And the Hivite, and the Arkite, and the Sinite,

And the Arvadite, and the Zemarite, and the Hamathite: and afterward were the families of the Canaanites spread abroad.

These peoples had practices common to their cultures that were destabilizing and destructive. When Israel was directed of God into the land of Canaan, which God promised they would inhabit, it was with the intention that they would displace the people and establish a healthy nation within the territory.

The Canaanite cultures practised human sacrifices; their rituals and religious practices included sacrificing their children with fire. Their most innocent and defenceless were subject to being sacrificed in order to satisfy their beliefs. The culture of the people was destructive and threatened their very existence. Yet, before the people of Canaan could implode, a new nation and a different people displaced them.

When the belief system, the values, the corporate thinking are wrong and ungodly, the very land is plagued. Yet, when the culture is productive and healthy, the land is blessed and prospers.

It is apparent that the Lord, with specific purpose, preserved the fruitfulness and fertility of the land of Canaan, in spite of the destructive cultures. For He had promised the Israelites that the land they would enter would be "flowing with milk and honey". He allowed their spies to see for themselves that the land was very good, and a place that they could prosper as a people. It was only by strict divine intervention that the land remained prosperous, flowing with milk and honey. (See Deuteronomy 11:12)

There is a direct relationship between a people and the land they occupy. Land responds to the ways of its inhabiting people. Whole ecosystems also are affected by the attitudes, mannerisms and values of a people.

{How great is the responsibility, therefore, of the leaders and governors of nations, for if they legislate and initiate improper practices within their nations, they 'soil' the very land.}

Proverbs 14:34

> *Righteousness exalteth a nation: but sin is a reproach to any people.*

Israel was uniquely protected by God, from both physical and spiritual foes. It prospered under the guidance of God and the leadership of David. As the people delved deeper and deeper into the ways of Zion they found more and more strength and blessings. The musicians and singers provided pleasant places for angelic hosts to lodge, and hostile territory to demons.

As with the impact of David's music within the palace walls when God allowed the evil spirit to trouble King Saul, so was the impact of the culture's music on the atmosphere. Evil spirits were likely evicted from the territory.

Those destructive negative beings that roam from place to place, stealing the joy and gladness from the hearts of men, would not have been permitted to function in Zion or in Israel.

The scriptures name some of these evil spirits that exist:

The spirit of jealousy
Lying spirits
Spirits of error
Spirits of infirmity
Dumb and deaf spirits
Spirits of whoredom
Spirits of divination and magic
Unclean spirits

These and other devils would have been under assault from the praises in Israel.

Psalm 76:2-3, 9-12

In Salem also is his tabernacle, and his dwelling place in Zion.

There brake he the arrows of the bow, the shield, and the sword, and the battle.

When God arose to judgment, to save all the meek of the earth

Surely the wrath of man shall praise thee: the remainder of wrath shalt thou restrain.

Vow, and pay unto the LORD your God: let all that be round about him bring presents unto him that ought to be feared.

He shall cut off the spirit of princes: he

is terrible to the kings of the earth.

The homes, the neighbourhoods, the communities, the cities would all have been refreshed, as the powerful culture affected and transformed every realm and sphere of the nation.

The principle of the power of praise over evil is a principle that all nations should recognize as they seek to increase peace and productivity in their borders. Music that is praise and worship to God purges the land of evil. Rejoicing in the One who is the source of all virtue and purity is a hostile action that evicts every spiritual being that is contrary to virtuous peaceful living. As praise and worship is offered to God, it declares that the participants validate and agree with the principles that exist in God –principles of righteousness, justice, love, integrity and peace.

Conviction by culture

Those persons who were not interested in the development strategy of the nation, nor in the music and dancing, those who were given to selfish ambition, and even those given to criminal activities, would doubtless have seen the blessings that individuals and families received as they became a part of the celebrating community.

The base persons of the land would likely have been convicted by the passion, sincerity, joy and reality of the relationship with God that the people enjoyed.

The needs of the people, individual and corporate,

were now being met. Unlike the old regime of King Saul, where the abused and afflicted found no justice and had to resort to camping with David in the wilderness, the innovations and creativity that came from the way of life presented by David prospered the people, so that abundance was everywhere, to be enjoyed by 'whoever would'.

The officials of the past regime would have been confronted by a revelation that they may have had to struggle with. Some would possibly have had a hard time converting to the radical new system of David, and the participation it required from them all.

This was the case with David's wife Michal, the daughter of Saul. She could not accept, or even fathom, David's behaviour and plans, but perceived his efforts to be childish and the frivolous acts of an insane commoner. She responded with hostility to David's demonstrative dancing unto God. Her disregard for David and his policies would, in the end, be to her own barrenness and bitterness.

{How easily men misjudge the individuality of those free to express themselves! They misunderstand the power of freedom, not having enjoyed it themselves. The bound find every occasion to scoff at those that are free, and find excuses for their own bondage, instead of challenging it and changing.}

Other relatives of King Saul, however, joined David and enjoyed the prosperity of his reign. For most of them, the surrendering of power, and that with passionate joy, was not an insurmountable challenge. They, too, prospered under King David's reign.

2Samuel 9:6-7

> *Now when Mephibosheth, the son of Jonathan, the son of Saul, was come unto David, he fell on his face, and did reverence. And David said, Mephibosheth. And he answered, Behold thy servant!*
>
> *And David said unto him, Fear not: for I will surely show thee kindness for Jonathan thy father's sake, and will restore thee all the land of Saul thy father; and thou shalt eat bread at my table continually.*

Though the strategy may have been unorthodox and unprecedented, its opponents could not argue with a system that clearly brought about the favour of God upon the people. It was obvious that Israel was a healthy nation, with a happy and blessed people.

Psalm 50:23

> *Whoso offereth praise glorifieth me: and to him that ordereth his conversation aright will I show the salvation of God.*

National stability

Due to the success of the strategy implemented in the city by King David, the nation of Israel flourished; no longer was Israel seen as a "struggling people", but as a strong nation.

Though the culture of the people created a stable

Israel, the occasional personal mistakes of King David did affect the land, and in one instance God had said trouble would result within his own home. His son Absalom attempted to overthrow him. It was a parenting error that had an unexpected backlash. While generally Israel was stable, the trouble that was to come to David's home spilled over and also affected the nation.

The few significant personal mistakes of the king did bring a rare slip in national development and stability at times. However, they were never too disastrous to jeopardize the power of the 'cultural project'.

Whatever the occasional incident, the nation advanced socially, economically and militarily. There was no nation at that time that threatened Israel's developmental advance.

The king himself, a former shepherd boy and 'wilderness' musician, had become astonishingly wealthy. From David's personal treasure he was able to donate to the national temple construction programme the equivalent of US$1.9 billion in gold and US$83 million in silver.

The other leaders of the nation, who themselves became tremendously wealthy, gave of their personal treasures the equivalent of US$2 billion in gold and US$120 million in silver.

1 Chronicles 29:2-9

> *Now I have prepared with all my might for the house of my God the gold for things to be made of gold, and the silver for things of silver, and the brass for things of brass, the iron for things of iron, and wood*

for things of wood; onyx stones, and stones to be set, glistering stones, and of divers colours, and all manner of precious stones, and marble stones in abundance.

Moreover, because I have set my affection to the house of my God, I have of mine own proper good, of gold and silver, which I have given to the house of my God, over and above all that I have prepared for the holy house.

Even three thousand talents of gold, of the gold of Ophir, and seven thousand talents of refined silver, to overlay the walls of the houses withal:

The gold for things of gold, and the silver for things of silver, and for all manner of work to be made by the hands of artificers. And who then is willing to consecrate his service this day unto the LORD?

Then the chief of the fathers and princes of the tribes of Israel, and the captains of thousands and of hundreds, with the rulers of the king's work, offered willingly,

And gave, for the service of the house of God of gold five thousand talents and ten thousand drams, and of silver ten thousand talents, and of brass

> *eighteen thousand talents, and one hundred thousand talents of iron.*
>
> *And they with whom precious stones were found gave them to the treasure of the house of the LORD, by the hand of Jehiel the Gershonite.*
>
> *Then the people rejoiced, for that they offered willingly, because with perfect heart they offered willingly to the LORD: and David the king also rejoiced with great joy.*

The nation had so prospered that large national gatherings were held; and at these gatherings there was public feasting sponsored by the monarchy. The nation's treasury also sponsored festivals at which the king ensured that every individual would have more than enough to eat and drink.

The national treasure was so strong it could fund the regular feasting of the entire nation and not go bankrupt.

When David thought to eventually make a more permanent structure for the housing of the ark, he planned that it would have only the most expensive building material and fixtures. The nation had enough resources to later embark on the construction of the enormous temple, where the interior was overlaid in purest gold.

Militarily, the nation had grown tremendously, and was able to subdue its arch-rivals, the Philistines. Israel subdued other nations as well; those who were hostile to them were overwhelmingly defeated, including Syria and Ammon.

David's generals and captains were renowned throughout the region because of their individual combat skills, and their military leadership skills. The influence of the culture was at work mightily on the entire nation.

Solomon comes

While David was yet living, he decided to hand the control of his successful kingdom over to one of his younger sons, Solomon. David's reign, in spite of the occasional personal errors, was noted as a greatly successful monarchy, and he passed on a truly successful and stable nation to Solomon to lead.

A regime's success can surely be measured on the basis of the successful systems that have been implemented for the people's well-being by their leadership; and David had proven that his policies and systems worked for the nation's benefit.

The young Solomon could have been an unstable man due to the circumstances surrounding his father and mother's marriage. David's relationship with Bathsheba, Solomon's mother, was as a result of one of his personal errors. Yet Solomon, in spite of the challenging situation, became the most qualified son of the king to take over leadership of Zion and the entire Israel.

{How often men meditate on their circumstances and forget their opportunities! It is unfortunate that so many allow their past to affect their future. The wise will leave the past in the past and passionately maximise their present and pursue a prosperous future.}

Solomon had personally benefited from his father's unique national development strategy. He was raised as a part of the Zion Culture. He was a young man of faith and passion and given to the arts.

Ecclesiastes 2:8

> *I gathered me also silver and gold, and the peculiar treasure of kings and of the provinces: I gat me men singers and women singers, and the delights of the sons of men, as musical instruments, and that of all sorts.*

He had a personal relationship with God, as did his father. He heard directly the counsel of God and did not have to always rely on the ministry of the prophets. He was passionate about God after the manner of David, his father, and was bold to express his devotion and love for God.

When Solomon began his reign, he took the nation to an even greater level of prosperity and stability. Under his leadership the nation would know unparalleled global influence and prosperity. Both the king and the people prospered tremendously.

1Kings 10:23-24, 27

> *So King Solomon exceeded all the kings of the earth for riches and for wisdom.*
>
> *And all the earth sought to Solomon, to hear his wisdom, which God had*

put in his heart.
And the king made silver to be in
Jerusalem as stones ....

Solomon continued the trend of his father, David, for many years. He presided over the construction of the temple, the more permanent facility that David had desired to construct.

(It is unfortunate that due to the elaborate nature of the building, the temple would eventually become more celebrated than God for whom it was constructed – a vice that would later cost the nation dearly.)

When the temple was completed it was dedicated in the customary ways of Zion – with music, singing and dancing. The sacrifice of animals was a part of the dedication as atonement for the people's sin, yet the primary offering of the people was their music, singing and dancing. The Lord responded to the offering of music and dancing with the manifestation of His presence through the Shekinah glory cloud; it hovered inside and over the temple. It was a sign to the people of God's presence, confirming again His being pleased with the nation and his covenanting to protect and bless them.

The people had never seen this scale of manifestation of the presence of God in their generation; the tremendous showing up of God's presence was only known to their foreparents at the birth of the nation.

It is within this atmosphere that God blessed Solomon with much greater wisdom and incredible leadership skill.

Solomon, as a product of the culture and a recipient of supernatural enabling, penned great and notable literary works. He authored most of the Book of Proverbs, and Ecclesiastes and The Songs of Solomon – poetic and prophetic masterpieces.

Dignitaries from all over the world came to visit Israel, to admire and learn from its systems and its success. One of the most prominent visitors to the nation was the Queen of Sheba. She came from a very wealthy nation herself, but was overwhelmed by the much greater level of prosperity she witnessed in Israel.

The Queen was overcome by the technology and the level of advancement she saw present in the nation, and in King Solomon.

1Kings 10:4-8

> *And when the queen of Sheba had seen all Solomon's wisdom, and the house that he had built,*
>
> *And the meat of his table, and the sitting of his servants, and the attendance of his ministers, and their apparel, and his cupbearers, and his ascent by which he went up unto the house of the LORD; there was no more spirit in her.*
>
> *And she said to the king, It was a true report that I heard in mine own land of thy acts and of thy wisdom.*
>
> *Howbeit I believed not the words, until I came, and mine eyes had seen it: and, behold, the half was not*

told me: thy wisdom and prosperity exceedeth the fame which I heard.

Happy are thy men, happy are these thy servants, which stand continually before thee, and that hear thy wisdom.

7

REBUILDING ZION

A New Work

WITH THE ADVENT OF THE Lord Jesus the times have changed and the functions on earth have intensified. Jesus Christ's coming has marked the 'end of the age' of earthly systems and patterns as known and esteemed by secular governments and individuals.

The misuse and mismanagement that have prevailed upon the earth have done significant damage to the earth's landscape, and to global animal and plant life.

God, through His Son, has begun to effect total restoration and transformation of the planet. The unprecedented destruction and pollution of the planet has warranted God's intervention. The processes of destruction which begun millennia ago, have now come to a head, and God has begun the end.

He has intervened to rescue mankind and the planet from corrupt, chaotic courses and destructive cultures. His intervention has initiated a new system of governance and leadership for the earth. He has appointed His most reliable and competent person to lead His governmental shift; His beloved Son Jesus shall reign as head of state to the earth.

As awareness of this truth bears upon men, hope returns to the earth – hope in the power and splendour of the reign of the Lord Himself. Because of Jesus, new passion and fervour find a place on earth. As a light at the end of the tunnel brings hope, so men of all nations are given a reason to celebrate.

Through God's grace, the continuous downward spiral has been challenged and changed, and prosperity and peace is being offered. In light of these truths, people from every nation and land who have been subject to injustices and hopelessness now have a tremendous reason to celebrate. And as they celebrate there is a glorious purpose and strategy unfolding within them.

The Spirit and the Son

Through David, the people of the Zion Culture were inspired to praise with the Ark of the Covenant, which represented the presence of God: yet, the people were also inspired to passionately praise because they were aware of the promises that were given them by God. One promise given to the nation was the coming of the Spirit of God to abide in the people of God: they praised in anticipation of this tremendous promise.

In this age the Holy Spirit has come, and the promise has been fulfilled.

The presence of the promised Spirit of God is now inspiring the ways of heaven on earth. The Holy Spirit has given those who have submitted themselves to Jesus' reign a taste of heaven's own culture – liberty, joy, and passion are being manifested in the earth again. The culture is on the rise again; and its powerful effect is being manifested.

Those who have truly yielded themselves to the rule and reign of the Son of God have been liberated to praise. They have been made free to explore their gifting and talents.

2Corinthians 3:17

> *Now the Lord is that Spirit: and where the Spirit of the Lord is, there is liberty.*

The expression of individuality is finding its place within those truly submitted to the lordship of the Son of God by faith. The Holy Spirit is revealing the fulfilled promises of God and their worth to God's people. He is inspiring passionate intimate arts – music, dancing and singing – through the revelation of the truth.

In eager anticipation of the reign of the Son of God over all the earth, the new era praisers have begun to sing. The new praisers have begun to be liberated to write songs, to play their instruments, to dance spontaneous dances and to choreograph unusual and expressive pieces. In anticipation and celebration of change everywhere and on every continent, The Zion Culture is arising. True worshippers are worshipping; New Testament praisers are singing by inspiration and empowerment of the Holy Spirit.

The Holy Spirit has begun to bring the effect of the anticipated reign of the new king. The power of the new Zion Culture has gone into effect; nations will begin to experience its transformative power, even as Israel did.

True worshippers

As the truth of transformation becomes more and more vivid to men, the passion of praise will become more and more intense. As the passion of praise becomes more and more intense, the power of transformation and change will begin to manifest. God has moved to facilitate a new period of praise, and a modern order of praise and worship.

John 4:23-24

> *But the **hour cometh, and now is**, when the true worshippers shall worship the Father in spirit and in truth: for the Father seeketh such to worship him.*
>
> *God is a Spirit: and they that worship him must worship him in spirit and in truth. [Emphasis added]*

God has initiated the reconstruction of ZION and the reformation of the Zion Culture. He has begun to rebuild the operation of the Zion Culture, yet with a modern flair.

The present construction will exceed the old by leaps

and bounds. For the old praisers praised in faith of that which they perceived to come – future promises. Yet, the new praisers praise from that which has come, that is, all God's promises; the promises of permanent blessings, unchangeable joy and eternal well-being. They praise regarding the fulfilled promise of heaven's best being given – God's Son and God's Spirit.

The new praisers praise from faith, experiential knowledge of God's love and revelation. They shall praise from the conviction of accomplished work. The

old praisers, as powerful as they were, praised from the confidence of God's love as seen through David and his passion; the new praisers will praise from confidence in God's love as seen through His Son's death, burial and resurrection. The old praisers praised after the order of the passion of King David; the new will praise after the order of the passion of Jesus Christ.

The revelation of permanence shall motivate unprecedented levels of passionate praise; for the 'kingdom' will not be given to a fallible son. It will not be handed over to a wise man, as Solomon; it is handed over to the infallible Son of God. His wisdom is unchanging and unending; He bears the omniscience of His Father, and has the eternal experience of all His father's ways.

(There is now no opportunity for error, as in the past; for the temple cannot be admired and adored above the God for whom it is created, for the intention is that the temple and the God of the temple shall be inseparable, one and the same.)

A new and higher level of passionate praise is arising in the earth, as the process of reconstruction and transformation of the planet has begun through Jesus

Christ. True Worshippers will see the entrance of the King to claim His praise and establish His people and the new governmental structure forever.

The New Testament True Worshippers – those prophesied of by the Lord –have begun to arise: a new people of passion, a new people of creativity and liberty. Passionate singers and songwriters, expressive dancers and musicians are arising – a new people of the arts.

A new foundation for Zion

A new foundation has been laid for the erection of a new Zion and the function of a new Zion Culture. The foundation laid is primarily spiritual, which erases the possibility of erosion by the elements, and facilitates its permanence. The foundation laid is now not geographical as much as it is relational.

The new foundation laid for the new Zion is a person: for geography is not priority but spirituality. The new Zion is being built and established on the basis of one man's reliability. God has chosen to erect the new Zion in a more permanent fashion. He is building Zion on His Son; for Jesus represents everything that the former place once represented, and more. Jesus represents a personal relationship with God; He represents freedom for individuals and wholehearted expressions of praise to God. Jesus is the solid foundation of the new Zion.

Isaiah 28:16

> *Therefore thus saith the Lord GOD,*
> *Behold, I lay in Zion for a foundation*
> *a stone, a tried stone, a precious*
> *corner stone, a sure foundation: he*

that believeth shall not make haste.

Jesus, therefore, is the foundation of the new culture. He is to be the inspiration and the foundation of the new strategy.

It is only a unique wisdom that would consider an individual more permanent than a geographic location. The reasoning defies logic and rationale, yet it is all God's wise plan.

Jesus represents the presence of God and the covenant of God. He also represents the meeting place of God, and the promises of God. The new culture is being established on the person of Jesus Christ – a more permanent arrangement. It is indestructible, unchangeable and irreversible. This was not the case with the Zion Culture of King David; for Solomon fell away from the system and Israel departed from the strategy.

The nation of Israel, after constructing the temple on a new location, fell away from the joys and focus of faith they had once found in Zion. The culture changed and reverted to one resembling the nations surrounding them; they adopted practices consistent with ordinary secular custom.

The Zion Culture of Jesus shall never change. The modern worshippers shall find an everlasting fortress which is guaranteed to remain. The centerpiece of the modern Zion Culture shall never be removed, as was the former; for in Israel they removed the Ark of the Covenant to what Solomon had thought to be a more permanent location, which proved to be an error for this greatly wise man.

God had spoken through the prophets to foretell the reconstruction of the order that David established.

Amos 9:11

> *In that day will I raise up the tabernacle of David that is fallen, and close up the breaches thereof; and I will raise up his ruins, and I will build it as in the days of old:*

God chooses to declare that He will raise up the Tabernacle of David again, and not the Tabernacle of Moses, for the delight was in that of David's. Yet, He refers to a more permanent arrangement than David could have ever constructed. It is called the Tabernacle of David for similarity of function, and not for similarity of construction. God has created the new place of praise for "whosoever would".

A new location that is special, and precedes its 'age', is prepared for the True Worshippers. The new Tabernacle of David will cause a flow superior to that of King David's. The earth is to be affected by the people in the vicinity of this new tabernacle: those who come close, those who will abide and reside in the Spirit, embracing the attitude of continual praise, they will affect the nations.

The old Tabernacle of David was furnished with the Ark of the Covenant as the centrepiece for inspiration to all the citizens of Zion. It worked successfully to the inspiration of the nation. Now the new tabernacle will have not an ark but a person as the centrepiece of inspiration for citizens. The praisers of old, inspired by the tabernacle and the ark, powerfully affected the entire nation of Israel; and now the new praisers and worshippers shall be inspired by the 'tabernacle' of the

Spirit, and they shall find in it Jesus Christ Himself. This entire arrangement was being foreshadowed by David and the then Zion Culture.

Acts 15:15-18

> *And to this agree the words of the prophets; as it is written,*
>
> *After this I will return, and will build again the tabernacle of David, which is fallen down; and I will build again the ruins thereof, and I will set it up:*
>
> *that the residue of men might seek after the Lord, and all the Gentiles, upon whom my name is called, saith the Lord, who doeth all these things.*
>
> *Known unto God are all his works from the beginning of the world.*

The new Zion experience

The strategy David was inspired to inject into the culture of the capital of Israel in his generation will be a strategy to be manifested by the Church in this generation.

As with Zion, the passion and the joy changed the social composition of the nation; so will the True Worshippers affect various nations and territories. As with Israel, so will the worshippers in the spirit facilitate transformation, prosperity, unity and stability.

Innovations will come to the modern Zion Culture worshippers. They shall be awash with creativity and inventions, as they are inspired while using the arts to express themselves passionately to God.

Those who oppose the system will have to contend with the realities of the joy, fulfilment, peace and love being experienced by those of the Zion Culture. Many will be convicted to convert, and will experience the power of the culture themselves.

Provisions and prosperity will be manifested on phenomenal levels within nations that have wholly adopted the Zion Culture. Supernatural production and national growth will be manifested. Sicknesses will be minimal within the nation, crime and violence shall be negligible, as the power of the culture affects the lands embracing it.

God shall, after a while, have Zion established on an international level, and it will be the only culture, the only experience on the planet.

Jesus of Judah

The Sovereign Father could have sent His Son to be born anywhere and at any time. He chose, with omniscient purpose, the age and place of Jesus' birth. He chose with omniscient wisdom the persons to parent His own Son. God chose Mary and Joseph, who both were direct descendants of King David, the former King of Judah and King of all Israel. God sent His Son to be born into a specific family and a specific territory, Bethlehem of Judah: 'Judea' in the New Testament. (Judah literally means 'Praise' in Hebrew.)

The Father aligned the birth of His Son and His physical lineage with the tribe of praise. It signifies that Jesus is aligned to the people of praise first. God has made Him to be the new King of Judah, the new King over praise. Though Jesus was to be the King of all creation, to indicate the importance of praise, God specifically associates Jesus' reign with Judah.

Jesus is called the Son of David for a purpose. He is seen as the rightful heir to the throne of King David, His forefather in the flesh. It is evident that this is so for the powerful work that David had accomplished in Zion and Israel, and the 'crowning' work that Jesus would do to bring what David had begun to fulfilment. Jesus is the King of Praise; He is the King of everything David sought to do for Zion and Israel.

Psalm 45:7

> *Therefore God, thy God, hath anointed thee with the oil of gladness above thy fellows.*

Spirituality before geography

It is amazing how it eludes us that simple spirituality affects entire societies. While the secular pursuits have remained material wealth, oil and gold, stocks and bonds, the answer for a nation to be successful has always been close at hand.

Nations have gone to war over meagre resources, and have ignored the greater values which are available to prosper their countries beyond their comprehension.

All people from every nation have been invited to Zion. Every nation and every land under heaven have been given a personal invitation from the Creator to come and adopt this culture of passion, to the well-being of their nation. No matter what the prevailing conditions are within any nation, any desperate situation is guaranteed to change with the manifestation of the powerful and influential Zion Culture.

Hebrews 12:22

> *But ye are come unto mount Zion, and unto the city of the living God, the heavenly Jerusalem, and to an innumerable company of angels*

If nations would but adopt the process of praise, the freedom of expression, the passion for dance, music, and songwriting in honour of the Lord Jesus Christ, their lands and their fortunes would change. For the same powers that delivered King Saul from evil spirits, and delivered the nation of Israel from surrounding enemies, would deliver their nations to progress and plenty.

Music is the joy of all men, and dancing comes naturally from birth, so the pursuit of the highest successes is made most simple and attainable to all mankind.

Apostle Paul, the New Testament writer, encouraged believers to manifest the strengths of the principles of the culture.

Ephesians 5:19-20

> *Speaking to yourselves in psalms and hymns and spiritual songs, singing and making melody in your heart to the Lord;*
>
> *Giving thanks always for all things unto God and the Father in the name of our Lord Jesus Christ*

As time winds down on the existing governmental structures, more individuals, and indeed nations, shall begin to adopt the Zion Culture. Entire islands shall be passionate praisers, and then will the end come, where the King of Kings will return to the earth and the system will be the order of the day. And as David foreshadowed the existence of the true Zion Culture, and the New Testament worshippers, even so did he foreshadow the return of the inspiration and joy of all men.

2Samuel 6:15

So David and all the house of Israel brought up the ark of the LORD with shouting, and with the sound of the trumpet.

Even so shall the King of Kings descend.

Revelation 14:1-3

And I looked, and, lo, a Lamb stood on the mount Sion, and with him an hundred forty and four thousand, having his Father's name written in their foreheads.

And I heard a voice from heaven, as the voice of many waters, and as the voice of a great thunder: and I heard the voice of harpers harping with their harps:

And they sung as it were a new song before the throne, and before[1] the four beasts, and the elders: and no man could learn that song but the hundred and forty and four thousand, which were redeemed from the earth.

8

LIFT UP YOUR HEADS

Open To God

As THE CHURCH AGE CONTINUES, may the leadership of the churches remain pliable in the hand of God. Once pliable, the operation of the Spirit will find its full expression upon the congregation. David warned:

Psalm 28:5

> *Because they regard not the works of the LORD, nor the operation of his hands, he shall destroy them, and not build them up.*

It is imperative that all be submitted to the rule and reign of the Lord Himself, and not attempt to subvert His leadership. As He leads, praisers will be manifest, and the arts will manifest as passion erupts for God. Personal leadership preference must give way to God's directions and operations.

As passion erupts, the young men and women who are hardly seen in the churches shall return, and must be facilitated; for they shall find with the new liberty the power and excitement that they seek in the house of the Lord.

Those who open up to the leadership of the Spirit shall experience an ever-increasing liberty; and an ever-increasing opportunity to explore their gifts and talents. The Holy Spirit shall bring the confidence and courage to the congregations of the Church to fully impact the nations with joy, love and wisdom.

The efforts of evangelism and missions now pursued will be seen as minuscule and mediocre in the light of the power of pure love and joy. The nations of the world will be forced to take another look at the Church. The purpose of missions has always been to bring the nations to worship God; we shall see worship bring the nations to the Church, as we open up to the Holy Spirit.

And now the Church must begin to throw off its religious robes and religious rituals and embrace real relationship with God. It must now abort the effort to look spiritual, and become truly spiritual.

{How few have grasped the knowledge that religiosity is not spirituality and spirituality is not religiosity: spirituality is living in 'reality'; for spirituality is power.}

Jesus long warned the Church regarding the dangers of hypocrisy in order to protect the power of the Church. He warned His leaders, the early church fathers, not to fall prey to the error of former Jewish leaders; for men have opted to abandon reality for pretence, choosing performances instead of participation.

After His ascension, the Lord continued to warn the pastors of the Church through John the beloved, on the isle of Patmos. Let us beware of an order of church that is not powerful and expressive. Let us not hinder or grieve the Spirit of God as He stirs the hearts of His people to freedom and expression.

Paul the Apostle warned the saints of the early church regarding a form of godliness and denial of the power thereof. Let the Church hear those warnings today.

However, God shall not be denied that which He seeks - True Worshippers.

We can do nothing against the truth, but for the truth, so allow me to be the first to welcome you to these days of refreshing; these days where worship will begin to take on a new dimension and new function on the earth.

Within these closing hours of the age, The Zion Culture shall propel the preparation of the Bride. No longer shall worship be a dated event, but it shall become an unending experience. Lift up your heads, as we welcome and witness the closing of the age, and indeed the end.